Through Washington's Eyes:
A Biographical Exegesis of Washington's Farewell Remarks Pertaining to Religion and Morality

Copyright

©2015 by Christopher R. Townsend

All rights reserved. No part of this book may be reproduced in any form, except the inclusion of brief quotations in review, without permission in writing from author/publisher.

ISBN-13: 978-1517247119

ISBN-10: 151724711X

"Scene at the Signing of the Constitution of the United States" by Howard Chandler Christy - The Indian Reporter. Licensed under Public Domain via Commons - https://commons.wikimedia.org/wiki/File:Scene_at_the_Signing_of_the_Constitution_of_the_United_States.jpg#/media/File:Scene_at_the_Signing_of_the_Constitution_of_the_United_States.jpg

Contents

Introduction

Why He Said It

      The Environment & Timing of the Address

      Global Response to Christendom

      The American Response to Christendom

      Faith and Reason in Revolutionary America

      Faith and the Founding Fathers

What He Said

      The Document

      Washington's Expression of Religion and Morality

      Washington's Apparent Religious Ambiguity

What It Means For Modern Americans

Conclusion

Bibliography

INTRODUCTION

The United States of America is at a tipping point. Politics seem to become more and more schismatic with each passing year. Each gavel strike of the Supreme Court appears to upset one group or another. Questions of morals have been shifting constantly and debates are reaching new levels of polarized aggression. At the foundation of these contentions is the fundamental and divisive debate over the church-state relationship. As with most political arguments, there is a tendency to focus on what is legally viable rather than what is beneficially applicable. In other words, rather than seeking the healthiest expression of church-state relations, opposing sides seem to simply jockey for extreme positions with the result being less of a wholesome balance and more of a never-ending pendulum swing of slander, harm, and discontent. Much of this argument, as it specifically pertains to legislating church-state relations, focuses on the original intent of the founding fathers. As such, it makes sense to consider seriously the position of those key revolutionary players.

In the formative years of the United States, in which many men and women of the period have been canonized in a sort of secular sainthood, when the original documents were being drawn up and redacted, President and General George Washington was considered to be "first in war, first in peace, and first in the hearts of his countrymen."[1] Of all American figures, perhaps none is more important and highly regarded than he. Even more, perhaps no literary work better encapsulates his wisdom than his Farewell Address. As the culmination of his experience, these were his parting words of love and warning to future generations of Americans. In his Farewell Address, President George Washington cautioned future generations of Americans that religion and morality are inextricably linked to the well-being of the USA; modern Americans would do well to heed his warning. To accurately capture the nuance of his message, why he said it, what he said, and what it means for modern Americans must all be considered. The result of this study captures the depth, value, and wisdom of Washington's forewarning. Americans should take seriously the implications of removing religion and morality from personal and public life.

---

[1] Joseph J. Ellis, Brotherhood of the Revolution (New York, NY: Fall River Press, 2012), 18.

Why He Said It:
How Washington's Environment Influenced Him to Speak

Historical documents present a problem for modern readers. With each passing year, the cultural distance between the original author and the modern audience grows wider. Disconnected from the original context, ancient messages are often reinterpreted and subsequently misconstrued in ahistoric idealism and confusion. To help recontextualize Washington's words, one must first paint a picture of the environment that birthed his message. If the elements of time and culture, for instance, have the potential to miscontextualize his meaning, it is the duty of the historian to see them recontextualized. Once this has been established, Washington's words can be more correctly recognized within the context of his understanding of religion and morality.

The Environment and Timing of the Address

George Washington was born at, and lived through, one of the most significant periods in history. His lifetime saw the rise and fall of nations, multiple revolutions, the founding of what would become the most powerful nation in the world, and countless other history-changing events. At the center of these changes was a shift in the Western perspective on the Church and religion.

Global Response to Christendom

The Post-Christian West had already begun to manifest as culturally normative in some senses. Centuries of ecclesiastic abuse had ravaged nations across the globe. The Church had split, and split again. Christians were murdered. Heathens were murdered. Kings and leaders were executed. Priests and theologians were excommunicated, some even as a postmortem attack on their character and beliefs. On a global stage, the Crusades brought to popular light the systematic failure of church-state relations. This international scandal was only exacerbated by centuries of Western colonization at the expense of natives, slave trades, and further ecclesiastic schisms. All of these events had occurred under the fallacious guise of Godly missions.

It is important to acknowledge that these outrages, though committed in the name of God, were regarded by many Christians of the day as evil. When nearly the entire European world was under Church authority, it stands to reason that all state activities would be regarded as inherently religious. Unfortunately, this included both good and bad efforts. It is easy to blame religion for these atrocities. It is easy, but inaccurate. The motivating factor was not religion, and many of the day recognized this fact. Nevertheless, it created a negative association with Christianity, one that is still being perpetuated today.

THE AMERICAN RESPONSE TO CHRISTENDOM

In response to the damages, several American colonies had been created as an escape from such tyrannical proceedings. The New World was an opportunity to meet God in a land unadulterated by church-state relations. Sadly, this ideal proved errant for many. Mankind, unable to escape its own nature, simply marred the new territory through the fire of old passions and familiar systems. During long periods of the 17th century, for example, Virginia was organized with the single doctrinal standard of the Church of England. Even the Puritans of the Massachusetts Bay Colony, who sought escape from England had no plans of creating a place for multiple religions or even multiple Christian denominations. Rather they sought a land in which they could establish a "pure church... free of opposition, distraction, and error."[2]

---

[2] Edwin S. Gaustad and Leigh E. Schmidt, *The Religious History of America*, rev. ed. (New York, NY: HarperOne, 2004), 54

Faith and Reason in Revolutionary America

Simultaneously, running just behind the Reformation, the Enlightenment produced a secular revolution. Medieval debates over faith and reason produced a class of elite intellectual extremists who began branding faith as archaic, superstitious, and increasingly unnecessary. Though atheism was not yet a widely accepted philosophy, naturalism began manifesting popularity. As Owen Chadwick notes about this period, "The Enlightenment was of the few. Secularization is of the many."[3] For these modernist elites, the superstitious supernatural needed to be stripped from the otherwise valuable notion of religious morality.

Faith and the Founding Fathers

Though a few major Revolutionary players were more moral deists than devout Christians, the opposite was true for others. The founding fathers were men holding to various views at both ends of the argument and everything in between. Even Thomas Paine, arguably the most aggressive religious dissenter of the group stated, "I believe in one God… and I hope for happiness beyond this life."[4] On the

---

[3] Mark A. Noll, *Turning Points: Decisive Moments in the History of Christianity*, 3rd ed. (Grand Rapids, MI: Baker Academic, 2012), 246.

[4] David Barton, *Original Intent: The Courts, the Constitution, and Religion*, 5th ed. (Aledo, TX: WallBuilder Press, 2008), 138.

other end, Patrick Henry strived to enact legislation that would see Christianity be "officially declared 'the established Religion of this Commonwealth."[5] The reason for this bill's rejection tells a great deal about the majority mindset of the founding fathers. As James Madison and Thomas Jefferson argued, if "Almighty God hath made the mind free… it follows then that humanity should do all it can to keep minds unshackled and uncoerced."[6] Such a statement is given context by Madison's personal experience with the religious state. At the age of twenty-two Madison, wrote to condemn that "diabolical, hell-conceived principle of persecution."[7] This statement was made following the recent arrests and beatings of Baptists by the Anglican Church of Virginia in 1774.

Washington grew up during a time of extraordinary passion in the conversation of religious liberties. He was leader among leaders. The founding fathers had the immense responsibility to set up a government system, which would better respond to the religious environment than any that had previously existed. The documents had been finished for

---

[5] Gaustad and Schmidt, 124.

[6] Gaustad and Schmidt, 125.

[7] Gaustad and Schmidt, 46

several years by the time Washington was leaving office. He now was in a place where he could begin making judgments about the environment that the founding documents would create.

What He Said:
Through the lens of Washington's upbringing and personal understanding of religion and morality

The Document

For over thirty years, the United States had called upon George Washington for service. First as a General, then as the President, he served faithfully, often as a sense of duty even if it was not conducive to his own personal desires. For most, his journey to New York, then the center of national government, was celebrated with parades, flowers, and speeches.[8] For Washington, it has been described as a funeral procession. He agreed to the presidency not out of personal ambition, but out of allegiance to the country.

As he was finishing his final duties as the first president, George Washington determined to provide generations of Americans with his collective wisdom. With the help of Alexander Hamilton and James Madison, Washington set out "to recommend to your frequent review, some sentiments which are the result of much reflection, of no inconsiderable observation, and which appear to me all-important to the

---

8 History of the World, 453.

permanency of your felicity as a people."[9] Religion was a major premise in his parting words:

> Of all the dispositions and habits which lead to political prosperity, religion and morality are indispensable supports. In vain would that man claim the tribute of patriotism, who should labor to subvert these great pillars of human happiness, these firmest props of the duties of men and citizens. The mere politician, equally with the pious man, ought to respect and to cherish them. A volume could not trace all their connections with private and public felicity. Let it simply be asked: Where is the security for property, for reputation, for life, if the sense of religious obligation desert the oaths which are the instruments of investigation in courts of justice? And let us with caution indulge the supposition that morality can be maintained without religion. Whatever may be conceded to the influence of refined education on minds of peculiar structure, reason and experience both forbid us to expect that national morality can prevail in exclusion of religious principle.[10]

---

9 Bill Kaufman, "Farewell George," The American Enterprise no. 74 (Mar 1996): accessed March 30, 2015, http://search.proquest.com.ezproxy.liberty.edu:2048/docview/225399466?pq-origsite=summon..

10 Washington.

Washington's first sentence highlights the primacy of this argument. "Of *all* [emphasis added] dispositions and habits," he says, "religion and morality *indispensable* [emphasis added]." He goes on to declare both religion and morality necessary characteristics of any patriotic perspective, claiming that subversion of either is nearly tantamount to treason. In a sort of prophetic warning to the future, Washington rebukes would-be atheists or amoralists claiming that anyone who tries to tear down these pillars is the antithesis of a patriot. His language is both beautiful and bold. He goes further still, to recognize that both religion and morality are vital characteristics of all civilians, regardless of influence or financial status. Again, recognizing the threat of atheism, Washington paints a bleak picture of a world without religion and morality declaring that without them there is no security for the very rights that Americans hold so dearly-property, reputation, and life. Finally, Washington rebukes philosophical assumptions of atheistic morality, suggesting only somewhat indirectly that the two (atheism and morality) are functionally incompatible: "Reason and experience both forbid us to expect that national morality can prevail in exclusion of religious principle."

Washington's words are unambiguous. Though, as will be seen shortly, Washington had a history of great etiquette regarding imposition of religion on others, he does not retreat in the least when bidding farewell to his adoring countrymen. Building line upon line, Washington, with the aid of Hamilton and Madison, boldly condemns the removal of religion from the national ethos.

Washington's Expression of Religion and Morality

Washington's Farewell address is pointed, if not entirely precise. Though Washington does not outline a legal definition of what he considers religion and morality to be, he gives some clue later in the document: "With slight shades of difference, you have the same religion, manners, habits, and political principles."[11] Speaking to the national populous, Washington, acknowledging the majority Judeo-Christian nation, split more by denomination than alternative gods, seems to suggest that it is some form of Christian religion to which he is referring in this Farewell Address.

Nevertheless, as he did not specifically define religion and morality, it is reasonable to seek further definition elsewhere. In other words, it is helpful to view external evidence of Washington's perspectives on religion and then compare them with the statements made within the address.

---

11 George Washington, "Washington's Farewell Address 1796," Yale's The Avalon Project, 2008, accessed May 1, 2015, http://avalon.law.yale.edu/18th_century/washing.asp.

This is made ever the more significant by the historic jockeying over Washington's faith.

Washington's Apparent Religious Ambiguity

Washington was markedly judicious with his public discourses on religion. Though there is good reason and intentionality behind his cautiousness, history has told many different stories about Washington's faith. For many, his use of phrases like Providence and Grand Architect suggest that he was not Christian at all. Instead, they suggest that he was more likely some form of deist or even uncommitted atheist. For others, the absence of reference specifically to Christ is seen as further evidence of Washington's deistic inclinations. A more careful study suggests that these conclusions are, however, more than slightly shortsighted. An historic consideration of Washington's life relationship with faith gives insight into his understanding of religion and morality, as presented in the Farewell Address.

Washington's Upbringing

George Washington came from a long line of devout men of God. Even within his own family, the reach of religious persecution stretched and scarred. The first Washington to arrive in the New World was John Washington, who fled "shame and financial hardship coming from religious persecution."[12] Interestingly, it was John's own father, a Puritan Minister, who condemned John for practicing Anglican Catholicism. The journey would shape George's upbringing. Being raised in Colonial Virginia, George was born into the Anglican faith to which his parents belonged.

As an adult, Washington had set prayers that he said each morning and evening. These prayers are decidedly Christian. They contain many references to Jesus Christ as the Son of God. He quotes directly from Scripture. He refers to this God as the God of His salvation.[13] Janice T. Connell captures the beauty of this reality, "Each American is the beneficiary of George Washington's prayers."[14]

Washington and Church

Whatever the nature of his public presentation of faith, on a personal level, record presents Washington as a devout and deeply religious man. Still, the primacy of Washington as The Father of this Nation has led many denominations to fight

---

[12] Janice T. Connell, The Spiritual Journey of George Washington (Charleston, SC: CreateSpace Independent Publishing Platform, 2013), 3.

[13] Connell, 33-49.

[14] Connell, 33.

over his membership.[15] He was baptized and married in the Anglican Church of Virginia, which was at the time the official church of the state.[16] He was born and raised Anglican, and was "buried with the full rites of the Anglican Church."[17] Throughout his life, he also attended and contributed to many other churches. What is clear, beyond any reasonable doubt, is that Washington was a regular participant, not only in personal expressions of faith, but also corporately through various church settings. The rites, rituals, and assemblies of the Church held a primary position in the birth, life, and death of George Washington.

Washington & His Public Expression of Faith

Claims to Washington do not only occur between Christian denominations, but secularists as well. While this may well be errant, it is not entirely without foundation. Whatever his personal faith may have been, Washington was exceedingly tactful in his communication, often to the point of ambiguity. Like many of his time, Washington preferred

---

15 Paul F. Jr. Boller, *George Washington and Religion* (Dallas: SMU Press, 1963), 1963, 25-26.

16 Boller, 26.

17 Connell, 5.

less confrontational terminology and appears to have cared a great deal about not offending.

Paul F. Boller, in a detailed study of George Washington's faith, notes that at one point, while writing to Indian (Native American) leaders, Washington crossed out the word "God" and replaced it with "The Great Spirit in the Sky."[18] His diplomatic nature can be seen in the sensitive consideration of his words. Washington's strikethrough is evidence of great respect for the beliefs of other peoples. To some, the word choice might appear syncretistic. However, when considered within the broader scope of Washington's character and treatment of faith, it becomes evident that the strikethrough was in fact far more a step toward amicable relations than syncretistic postulations.

Nevertheless, while he took care not to offend other leaders, Washington clearly valued the Christianity of his upbringing and personal preference. In a speech to Delaware chiefs in 1779, he stated, "You will do well to wish to learn our ways of life, and above all, the religion of Jesus Christ. This will make you a greater, happier people than you are."[19] This elevation of the Christian faith is made exponentially more potent in the overall picture of Washington's great

---

18 Boller, 69.

19 Boller, 68.

linguistic care about religion. For him to make such a bold claim to a group that held to a non-Christian belief system was not his norm. Generally unwilling to make such evangelistic suggestions, Washington shows a rare example of stepping out of his common etiquette.

Even in the midst of war, the primacy of Christianity can be seen in his commands. "While we are zealously performing the duties of good Citizens and soldiers, we certainly ought not to be inattentive to the higher duties of Religion. To the distinguished character of Patriot, it should be our highest Glory to add the more distinguished Character of Christian."[20] Washington, who clearly viewed patriotism as a most noble aspiration, places Christianity as the pinnacle of character. Another soldier writes, "The General [Washington] hopes and trusts, that every officer and man, will endeavor so to live and act as becomes a Christian Solider."[21]

As attested to by his own words, actions, and the biographies of countless early authors, President George Washington was a man of great faith in Christ. This faith, like many of his peers, if they can be called that, impressed upon him the importance of liberty for all. It appears from record, that he generally took great care in not offending the views of

---

20 Boller, 69.

21 Connell, 32.

others. For those under his command, however, Washington felt it his duty to guide. This guidance, according to Washington's own words, naturally directed toward the faith and morality associated with Christianity. Though he felt it not his place to impose his religion on others, such as the Native Americans, he saw in Christianity an unparalleled value, capable of bringing people to a higher calling of goodness and peace. He felt this way despite being born into a world torn apart by Christian sects, theocracies, and atrocities done in the name of God. Repeatedly throughout his life, George Washington expressed to those he lead his belief that religion and morality are inextricably linked to patriotism, public felicity, and protection of property. More accurately, statements within the document, as well as Washington's history with faith, seem to suggest that it is specifically Christianity to which he refers.

What It Means Today:
Viewing Modern Hostilities through Washington's Words

Washington recognized that consequences exist beyond the formal legal system. His comments about morality operating in exclusion of religion are not just a suggestion about legislation; his statements recognize the power of the people. Washington understood the limitations of government. He understood that while it was the government's duty to provide a free and protected environment, true national freedom can only be obtained when the population as a whole recognizes the value of these two indispensable pillars.

Andy Crouch, in his lecture on Religious Freedom and the Common Good, captures the significance more explicitly when he describes two ways in which religious freedom can be restricted within a geopolitical culture, what he calls government restriction and social hostility. "Americans tend to think of religious freedom as a legal or governmental matter, but social hostility is just as important."[22] Crouch suggests that the law is only one aspect required for religious freedom. The other portion involves the character and treatment of people, especially religious minorities, within the private sector. "The test of religious freedom is how it protects religious minorities."[23] This includes the way people treat one another beyond the minimal requirements of the law. Crouch goes on: "If you care about the flourishing of persons,

---

22 Andy Crouch, "Religious Freedom and the Common Good" (video of lecture, Q Ideas 2015, posted April 1, 2015), accessed May 2, 2015, https://www.youtube.com/watch?v=W3-rq3cl5uo.

23 Washington.

especially the vulnerable in a community, you will care about freedom of religion."[24]

Washington understood these elements were requisite for national felicity. The government will only reflect the values of the people, as it is they who produce the government. Therefore, it is vital that people have a moral foundation from which they govern. Moreover, philosophically Washington recognized that morality becomes relative without a higher power. Though Nietzsche had not yet penned his famous words, Washington already understood the reductionist elements of relative morality.

The founding fathers had been reared in a culture with great religious and governing uncertainty. Coming from centuries of religious oppression, and even seeing the same structures manifest in the New World, these men sought to create a new system which would protect against religious imposition. Often this is confused in modern American culture. Without proper understanding of the historical context, statements like "separation of church and state" can come across as anti-religious. Justice William Rehnquist regarded this as "a misleading statement."[25]

---

24 Washington.

25 Barton, 49.

Somehow, to many modern minds, "separation of church and state" has come to mean freedom from religion rather than freedom of religion, meaning that people should not be subject to witnessing alternative expressions of faith. Religion should become entirely private according to some. Public displays of faith or belief are taboo and unwelcome. These matters become ever more complicated in arenas such as public education. What is an acceptable use of public funds, for example? What is not? These questions are immensely difficult to answer in pluralistic societies with protection of religion, such as the one found in the United States, a far more religiously diverse country than existed in Washington's time.

Attempting to perfectly apply Washington's words to all modern situations is an unsafe gamble. There is no way to prove exactly what he meant. The best that can be accomplished is an educated estimation. Generally, however, certain principles can be extracted from his words. These principles can then be applied to modern situations, not as divine law might be, but rather as the words of a fatherly ancestor of immense wisdom, experience, and passion. These principles can likely be used within the legal system of government restriction, but they must become lessons in the arena of social hostility. With all the background considered, Washington's words can now be applied to modern society.

Firstly, recognize that religion and morality are paramount to political success. "Of all the dispositions and habits which lead to political prosperity, religion and morality are indispensable supports."[26] Without both of these elements, the political system will fail. Political parties divide America. Corruption has reached new levels of debasement, if not in principal, then certainly in influence . The past year has seen nationwide riots erupting in violence. As Washington's words warned, the political systems of America are failing at an unprecedented rate. This is not a problem limited to the government sector. As religion has grown out of favor, so too has morality. The system is breaking just as Washington prophesied.

So strongly did Washington feel about the relationship between religion and morality and political prosperity that he reminds Americans, past, present, and future that if one is to be for their country, they must also be for religion and morality. "In vain would that man claim the tribute of patriotism, who should labor to subvert these great pillars of human happiness, these firmest props of the duties of men and citizens."[27] Growing anti-American sentiment seems to be accompanying the religious upheaval. A loss of national

---

26 Washington.

27 Washington.

identity has led to resurgent conflict and violence dividing black and white, Republican and Democrat, religious and irreligious.

Certainly, this environment cannot be blamed exclusively on atheism. After all, many of these problems existed in the more religious environment even prior to the Revolution. However, note that Washington sets up religion as a foundation to morality. It is not that he suggests religion guarantees morality, only that morality will not prevail without religion. Then, without either, nations will fall.

It is up to each and every man, woman, and child to hold fast to these religious and moral foundations. "The mere politician, equally with the pious man, ought to respect and to cherish them. A volume could not trace all their connections with private and public felicity."[28] Notice how Washington suggests that religion and morality transcend both the private and public well-being. Here, despite the separation of church and state, he recognizes the role these elements play within the government. Contrary to the rhetoric of those who would see the state free from religion, Washington warns that the value of religion and morality are beyond measure.

If freedom of religion protects the liberties of a nation's inhabitants, freedom from religion is sure to rob them of the

---

28 Washington.

same freedoms. "Let it simply be asked: Where is the security for property, for reputation, for life, if the sense of religious obligation desert the oaths which are the instruments of investigation in courts of justice?"[29] How clear are his words. Just as Christ proclaimed that the law and prophets hang upon the commands to love God and neighbor, so too does Washington suggest that the proper exercise of the state law depends upon religion. Recall as well that Washington, on more than one occasion, suggested that the superior form of religion was that of the Christian ilk. Modern Americans must not impose religion on others, but attempts to remove Christianity from its historic place in the US government are tantamount to deprivation of rights.

Many modern atheists, especially those of the New Atheism, proclaim loudly that religion is not needed for morality. Some even go so far as to declare religion antithetical to morality. This argument is not only philosophically fallacious, experience also shows the dangers of such beliefs. "And let us with caution indulge the supposition that morality can be maintained without religion. Whatever may be conceded to the influence of refined education on minds of peculiar structure, reason and

---

[29] Washington.

experience both forbid us to expect that national morality can prevail in exclusion of religious principle."[30]

---

[30] Washington.

Conclusion

Washington grew up in the years leading up to the American Revolution. It was a tumultuous period both politically and religiously, nationally and internationally. Coming out of the Reformation and in the midst of the Enlightenment the world was abuzz with a mix of theories, ideologies, and new religions. After one of the most historically successful careers as both General and national leader, Washington, with two of his cabinet members, set out to create a document that would guide the USA for generations to come. The twenty-first century has seen the fulfillment of many of Washington's predictions. Considering the confusion and loss of national identity that pervades American culture today, citizens and politicians alike can surely glean wisdom from the First President's cautions. In his Farewell Address, Washington describes religion and morality as indispensable supports. An historic consideration of his words and experiences suggest that, by religion and morality, Washington means to ingratiate the people of the United States to the moral and religious systems of Christianity. As America is being blown about in storms of political and religious division, it would be wise to anchor modern movements back to these bold and profound words from George Washington. In his Circular to the States, Washington reminds Americans that the responsibility belongs entirely to them, "The United States came into being as a Nation, and if their citizens should not be completely happy, the fault will be entirely their own."[31]

---

[31] Connell, 85.

Bibliography

Barton, David. *Original Intent: The Courts, the Constitution, and Religion.* 5th ed. Aledo, TX: WallBuilder Press, 2008.

Boller, Paul F. *George Washington and Religion.* Dallas: Southern Methodist University Press, 1963. Accessed March 31, 2015. http://babel.hathitrust.org/cgi/pt?id=mdp.39015009203103;view=1up;seq=11.

Coffin, Charles Carleton. *The Story of Liberty.* Gainesville, FL: Maranatha Publications, 1987.

Connell, Janice T. *The Spiritual Journey of George Washington.* Charleston, SC: CreateSpace Independent Publishing Platform, 2013.

Crouch, Andy. "Religious Freedom and the Common Good." Q Ideas. Posted April 1, 2015, Accessed May 2, 2015, https://www.youtube.com/watch?v=W3-rq3cI5uo.

Ellis, Joseph J. *Brotherhood of the Revolution.* New York, NY: Fall River Press, 2012.

Hall, John Whitney. *History of the World: Earliest Times to the Present Day.* North Dighton, MA: JG Press, 1997.

Kaufman, Bill. "Farewell George." *The American Enterprise* (Mar 1996). 74. Accessed March 30, 2015. http://search.proquest.com.ezproxy.liberty.edu:2048/docview/225399466?pq-origsite=summon.

Lane, Tony. *A Concise History of Christian Thought.* Revised ed. Grand Rapids, MI: Baker Academic, 2006.

Lengel, Edward G., ed. *A Companion to George Washington.* Malden, MA: Wiley-Blackwell, 2012. Accessed March 31, 2015. http://rx9vh3hy4r.search.serialssolutions.com/?

ctx_ver=Z39.88-2004&ctx_enc=info%3Aofi%2Fenc
%3AUTF-8&rfr_id=info:sid/
summon.serialssolutions.com&rft_val_fmt=info:ofi/
fmt:kev:mtx:book&rft.genre=book%20item&rft.title=A
+Companion+to+George+Washington&rft.au=Lengel%2C
+Edward+G&rft.atitle=Religion%3A+George
+Washington%2C+Anglican+Gentleman&rft.pub=Wiley
%E2%80%90Blackwell&rft.isbn=9781444331035&rft.spa
ge=558&rft.epage=575&rft_id=info:doi/
10.1002%2F9781118219935.ch32&rft.externalDocID=10.
1002%2F9781118219935.ch32&paramdict=en-US.

Noll, Mark A. *Turning Points: Decisive Moments in the History of Christianity*. 3rd ed. Grand Rapids, MI: Baker Academic, 2012.

Peters, Gerhard, and Woolley, John T., eds. *Presidency A to Z*. Washington DC, USA: SAGE Publications Inc. (US), 2012. Accessed March 30, 2015. http://
rx9vh3hy4r.search.serialssolutions.com/?
ctx_ver=Z39.88-2004&ctx_enc=info%3Aofi%2Fenc
%3AUTF-8&rfr_id=info:sid/
summon.serialssolutions.com&rft_val_fmt=info:ofi/
fmt:kev:mtx:book&rft.genre=book
%20item&rft.title=American+Government+A+to+Z%3A
+The+Presidency+A+to+Z&rft.atitle=Farewell
+Addresses&rft.date=2012-01-01&rft.pub=CQ
+Press&rft.isbn=9781608719082&rft.externalDocID=109
52160&paramdict=en-US.

Washington, George. "Washington's Farewell Address 1796." Yale's The Avalon Project. 2008. Accessed May 1, 2015. http://
avalon.law.yale.edu/18th_century/washing.asp.

Made in the USA
Charleston, SC
19 September 2015